Walter Foster
Jr.

learn to draw
Dogs &
Puppies

Step-by-step instructions for
more than 25 different breeds

ILLUSTRATED BY ROBBIN CUDDY

Table of Contents

Tools & Materials

There's more than one way to bring your furry friends to life on paper—you can use crayons, markers, or colored pencils. Just be sure you have plenty of good "dog colors"—black, brown, and white, plus yellow, orange, and red.

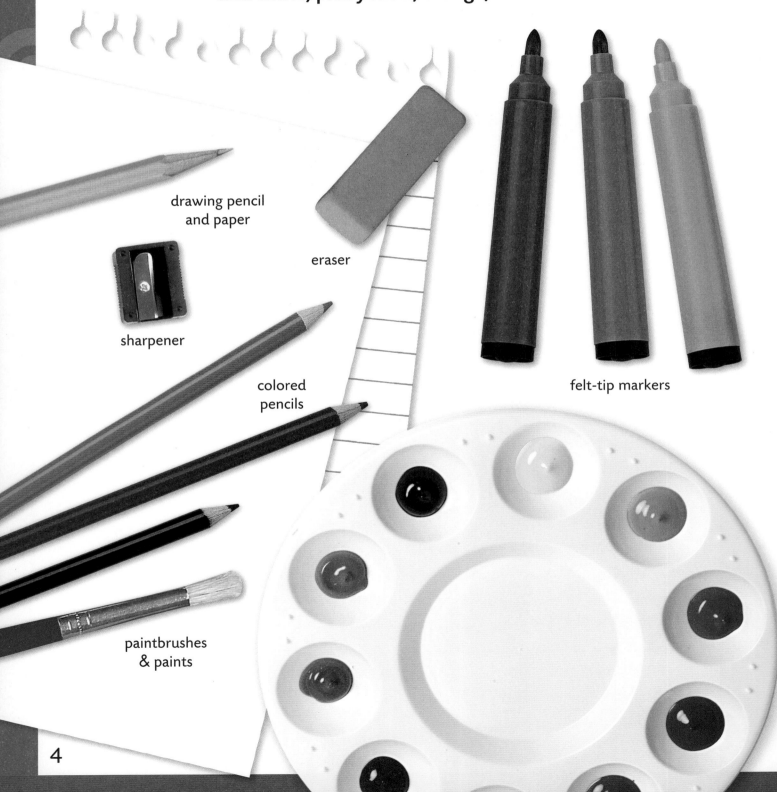

drawing pencil and paper

eraser

sharpener

colored pencils

felt-tip markers

paintbrushes & paints

How to Use This Book

The drawings in this book are made up of basic shapes, such as circles, triangles, and rectangles. Practice drawing the shapes below.

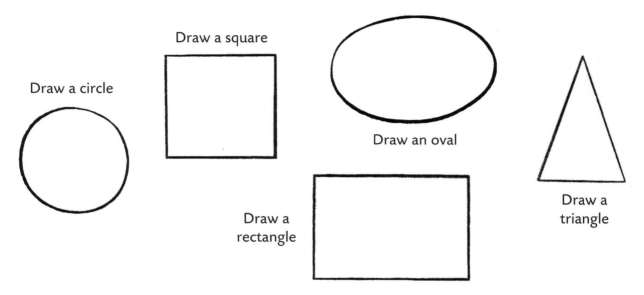

Draw a circle

Draw a square

Draw an oval

Draw a rectangle

Draw a triangle

Notice how these drawings begin with a basic shape.

In this book you'll learn about the size, color, origin, and personality of each featured dog breed. Look for mini quizzes along the way to learn new and interesting facts!

Look for this symbol, and check your answers on page 64!

Breeds

Dog breeds range widely in size, appearance, and personality. There are more than 170 different dog breeds!

Did you know?

The height of a dog is measured from the top of its shoulder down to its feet.

Breeds are classified into different groups, which describe a dog's behavior, skills, or size.

Standing as short as 6 inches from the shoulder to the ground, the Chihuahua is one of the world's smallest dog breeds.

The Puli has a long, corded coat.

The Sharpei is known for its loose skin and wrinkled appearance.

The tall, skinny Greyhound can reach speeds of more than 30 miles per hour.

Standing as tall as 35 inches from the shoulder to the ground, the Great Dane is one of the world's tallest dog breeds.

Coats

Below are a few different terms commonly used to describe a dog's coat, or fur. Refer to this guide as you learn to draw!

Roan is a hair color that shows a mix of white hairs with another color.

Blue merle is a hair pattern that shows black markings within blue-gray hair. The markings can be spots or streaks. Dogs can also be *red merle*.

Brindle is a hair pattern that shows subtle black "stripes" within another color.

Fawn is a shade of brown that leans to a golden red.

Harlequin is a hair pattern that shows black or gray spots within white hair. These markings vary widely in size.

Blue is a hair color that appears blue-gray.

Boxer

Height:
21–25 inches
Weight:
60–70 lbs

Colors: White and
fawn, or brindle
with a black mask

Coat:
Short

Group:
Working

Did You Know?

Boxers are born
with triangular ears
that flop forward, but
some owners "crop"
them so they
stand upright.

The Boxer is a large-pawed watchdog with a square muzzle, a square body, and an underbite.

Pup Personality

- energetic
- cheerful
- alert

1

2

3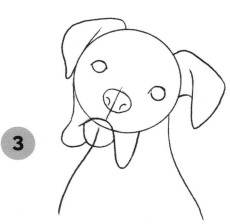

4

5

6

Basset Hound

Did You Know?

Bassets have easygoing, loving personalities, but can also be mischievous. Known as the "clown" of the canine world, they love to "sing!"

Basset Hounds have loose skin on the face that droops around the eyes, giving them a sad, yet loveable expression.

Pup Personality

- sweet
- devoted
- tenacious

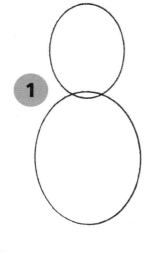

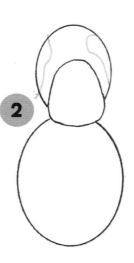

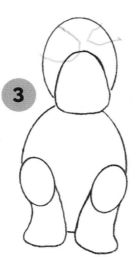

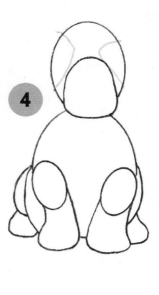

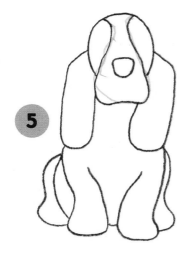

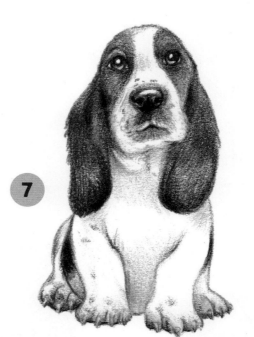

Dalmatian

Group:
Non-Sporting

Height:
19–23 inches
Weight:
50–55 lbs

Color: White with
dark spots

Coat:
Short

Fun Fact!

Once known for escorting horse-drawn carriages in the 18th century, including fire engines, the Dalmatian earned the nickname "Fire House Dog."

Dalmatians are intelligent dogs with speed, stamina, and impressive memories.

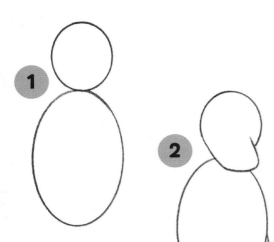

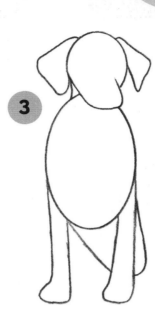

Chihuahua

Height:
5–9 inches
Weight:
Up to 6 lbs

Group:
Toy

Color: Black, chocolate, fawn, white, or blue

Coat:
Long or short

Fun Fact!

Ancient Aztec rulers considered the Chihuahua's ancestors good-luck charms!

These tiny dogs with big eyes, ears, and personalities are one of the smallest breeds in the world!

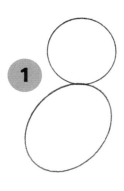

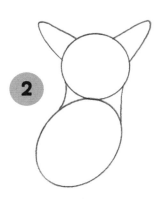

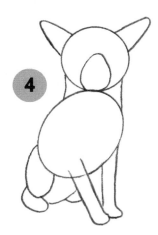

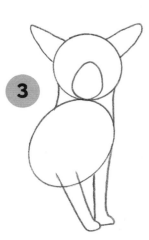

Pomeranian

Group:
Toy

Height:
6–7 inches
Weight:
3–7 lbs

Colors: White,
black, brown,
orange, and
reddish-brown

Fun Fact!

famous "Pom" owners include the composer Mozart and artist Michelangelo, whose Pomeranian is said to have sat and watched him paint the ceiling of the Sistine Chapel.

Coat:
Long

This spunky breed has a curled tail and a thick, fluffy coat that gives it an adorable rounded shape. Some say the "Pom" looks like a teddy bear.

Can you guess what other fluffy, outgoing dog the Pomeranian is related to?

(Answer on page 64)

Mini Quiz

Beagle

Breed Details

Group: Hound
Height: 13–16 inches
Weight: 18–30 lbs
Coat: Short
Colors: White, black,
brown, tan,
fawn, red, and blue

Did You Know?

Originally bred as
hunting companions,
Beagles have an amazing
sense of smell and
remarkable howling
ability.

This compact hound has a cheerful, energetic personality that makes it a popular family pet.

Who is the world's most famous cartoon Beagle? (Answer on page 64)

Mini Quiz

Dachshund

Breed Details

Group: Hound
Height:
Standard, 7–10 inches;
Miniature, under 7 inches
Weight:
Standard, 16–32 lbs;
Miniature, up to 11 lbs
Coat: Smooth, wire,
or long
Colors: Black, chocolate, tan,
cream, red, and blue

Did You Know?

The Dachshund's distinctive shape has earned it nicknames such as "weiner dog," "sausage dog," and even "hot dog."

Originally bred to hunt badgers, today this short-legged breed makes a loyal companion.

Pup Personality

- playful
- stubborn
- clever

1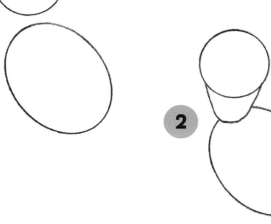

2

3

4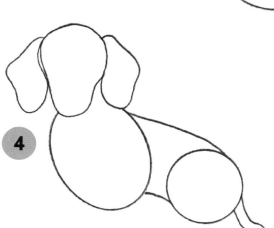

5

6

7

21

Bulldog

Breed Details

Group: Non-Sporting
Height: 13–15 inches
Weight: 40–50 lbs
Coat: Short
Colors: White, black, red, and fawn

Did You Know?

Originally bred to fight bulls hundreds of years ago in Europe, these brave dogs are also called "English Bulldogs."

Bulldogs have a stocky build, large head, and folded ears. Its unique face features a flat muzzle and an endearing overbite.

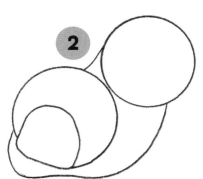

Pup Personality

- gentle
- outgoing
- friendly

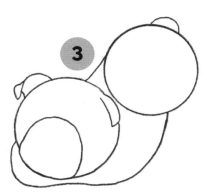

German Shepherd

Group:
Herding

Height:
22–26 inches
Weight:
75–95 lbs

Colors: Black
and tan, or
black and gray

Coat:
Short inner hair
and medium-long
outer hair

Fun Fact!

German Shepherds are often used as service dogs. The first seeing-eye dog and the first dog to receive a military medal were both German Shepherds!

These large, muscular dogs are often chosen for military and police work, but German Shepherds also make loving, loyal family pets.

Pup Personality

- intelligent
- watchful
- obedient

1

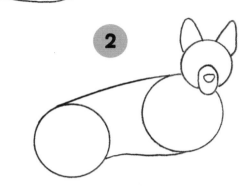

2

3

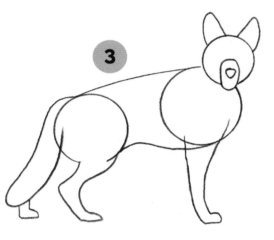

4

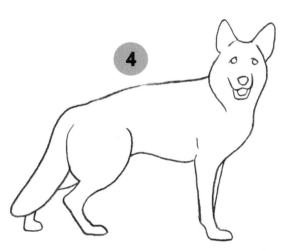

5

6

Labrador Retriever

Height:
21.5–22.5 inches
Weight:
55–75 lbs

Group:
Sporting

Colors:
Yellow, black,
or brown
(chocolate)

Coat:
Short

Fun Fact!

Along with other retriever breeds, Labrador Retrievers are said to have "soft mouths" gentle enough to carry a raw egg without breaking it!

Originally bred as fishing and hunting companions, Labs are now a very popular breed for families.

Pup Personality

- active
- friendly
- eager

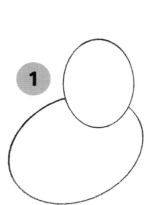 1

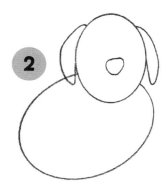 2

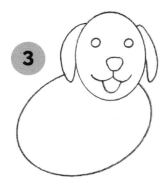 3

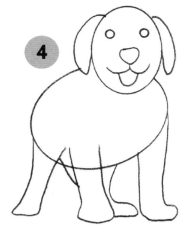 4

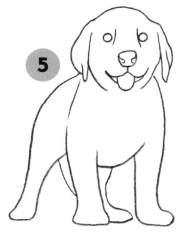 5

 6

 7

Akita

Breed Details

Group: Working
Height: 24–26 inches
Weight: 75–110 lbs
Coat: Thick, double coat of medium length
Colors: Any color, but often sable and white; can be brindle and pinto

Akitas are originally from Japan, where they are one of seven breeds designated as a national monument.

Fun Fact!

With a round face, furry body, and forward-folding ears, Akitas are known for their loyalty and courage.

True or false: Akitas were originally bred as hunting dogs in Japan.

(Answer on page 64)

Mini Quiz

1

2

3

4

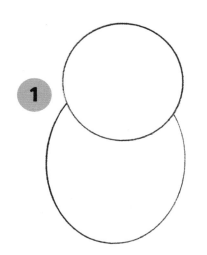

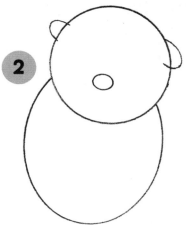

5

6

7

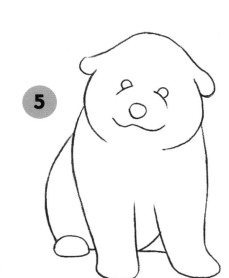

Australian Shepherd

Height:
18-23 inches
Weight:
35-70 lbs

Colors:
Black or red
merle; black or
red, with
or without
white markings

Group:
Herding

Coat:
Wavy or straight,
medium-length hair

Called "Aussies"
for short, these dogs
have many names!
Australian Shepherds
are also known as
Pastor dogs, Spanish
Shepherds, and Bob-
Tails, among others.

**Fun
Fact!**

These dogs are very agile and show great stamina. Devoted to their families, Australian Shepherds also make wonderful guard dogs.

Pup Personality

- active
- even-tempered
- shy

Yorkshire Terrier

Group:
Toy

Height:
8–9 inches
Weight:
Up to 7 lbs

Colors:
Puppies are black and tan; adults are blue and tan

Coat:
Long

Fun Fact!

This breed comes from the Yorkshire county of England, where they were originally used to hunt rats!

Called "Yorkies" for short, these dogs are known for their silky hair that grows long as they mature, sometimes flowing to the ground.

Pup Personality

- independent
- bold
- intelligent

1

2

3

4

5

6

Cocker Spaniel

Breed Details

Group: Sporting
Height: 14–15 inches
Weight: 22–29 lbs
Coat:
Medium length,
flat or wavy
Color:
Wide variety

Did You Know?

There are two officially recognized Cocker Spaniel breeds—English and American. The English breed is slightly larger than the American breed and has a longer snout.

Originally bred as a bird-hunting companion, these silky-haired dogs have low, floppy ears and tails that wiggle with excitement!

Pup Personality

- sociable
- trusting
- even-tempered

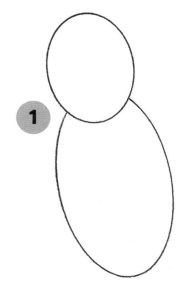

1

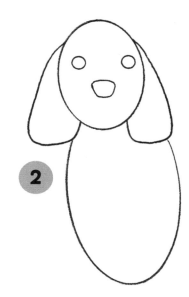

2

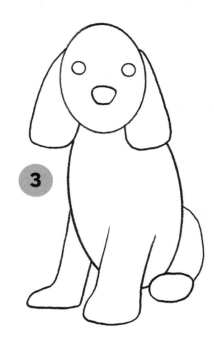

3

4

5

6

Pembroke Welsh Corgi

Group:
Herding

Height:
10–12 inches
Weight:
25–38 lbs

Colors:
Red, blue, sable, fawn, black and tan, or black and white; some have white markings

Fun Fact!

There are two types of corgis: the Pembroke Welsh and the Cardigan. The Cardigan Corgi is a bit taller with a longer tail and larger ears.

Coat:
Short to medium in length

These low-to-the-ground farm dogs have large, erect ears that point outward, creating a distinct triangular head shape.

Pup Personality

- obedient
- friendly
- bold

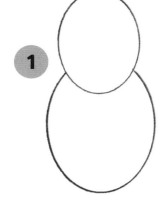
1

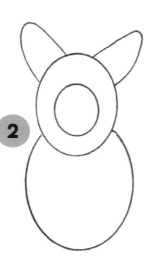
2

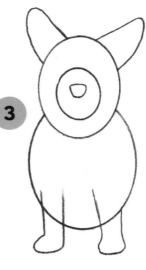
3

4

5

6

7

Poodle

Breed Details

Groups: Non-Sporting (Standard and Miniature Poodles) and Toy (Toy Poodle)
Height: Standard, above 15 inches; Miniature, 10–15 inches; Toy, under 10 inches
Weight: 7–70 lbs
Coat: Long in length; curly mix of woolly and wiry
Color: White, black, apricot, gray, cream, or brown

Did You Know?

The Poodle is the national dog of France, but it originated in Germany. The name "Poodle" comes from the German word *pudel*, which means to splash in the water.

Poodles have a proud, royal apprearance. Their hair is often clipped into fancy shapes that strategically help keep them warm, as well as stay afloat in water!

Mini Quiz

True or false:
Poodles do not
shed any hair.
(Answer on page 64)

Pug

Breed Details

Group: Toy
Height: 10–11 inches
Weight: 14–18 lbs
Coat: Short
Color:
Black, silver fawn,
or apricot fawn with
a black mask

Did You Know?

The Pug is one of the oldest dog breeds in history! Many European royals have kept Pugs as pets since the 16th century.

With its small, curled tail; large head; wrinkles; big eyes; and wide muzzle, the pug makes an adorable family pet.

Pup Personality

- playful
- affectionate
- smart

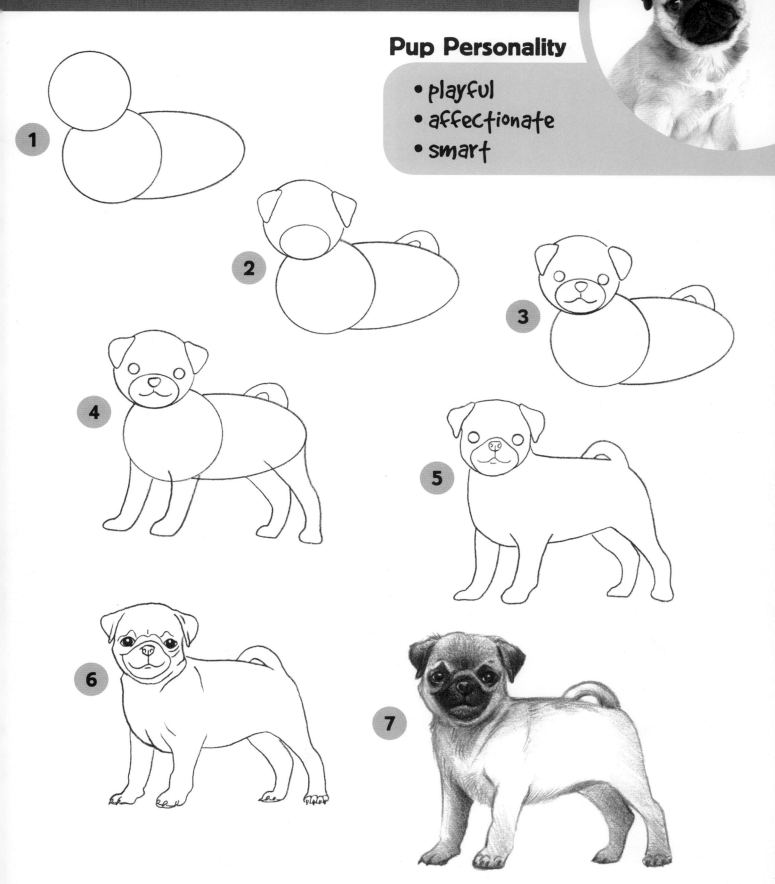

Siberian Husky

Group:
Working

Height:
20–23.5 inches
Weight:
35–60 lbs

Colors:
Black, white,
gray, or tan

Coat:
Medium-length
with a soft
undercoat and
smooth overcoat

Fun Fact!

Siberian Huskies
have been herding
reindeer in Siberia
for more than
3,000 years!

Originally bred as a sled dog, the Husky has mask-like head markings, upright ears, and a dense coat that keeps it warm in the snow.

1

2

3

4

5

6

7

Mini Quiz

Huskies are known for their beautiful piercing eyes. What color are they?
A. blue
B. brown
C. both
(Answer on page 64)

Scottish Terrier

Breed Details

Group: Terrier
Height: 10 inches
Weight: 18–22 lbs
Coat:
Medium to long in
length; wiry
Color:
Black, brindle, or
wheaten

Did You Know?

Despite its small
size, the Scottie is
frequently used as a
mascot for schools and
colleges because of its
fearless nature!

Called "Scottie" or "Scottie Dog" for short, these compact dogs love to dig and chase.

Scotties are often seen wearing a traditional Scottish print on their collars, bows, or accessories. Do you know what it is?

(Answer on page 64)

Mini Quiz

45

Maltese

Height:
About 5 inches
Weight:
Less than 7 lbs

Coat:
Long

Group:
Toy

Colors:
White, white
with lemon, or
white with tan

Fun Fact!

The Maltese gets
its name from an
island off the coast of
Italy called "Malta,"
which is considered its
birthplace.

These tiny dogs have light hair and dark, round eyes. The Maltese has been a favorite pet among royals for centuries.

Pup Personality

- tidy
- affectionate
- lively

Miniature Pinscher

Group:
Toy

Height:
10–12.5 inches
Weight:
8–10 lbs

Colors:
Red, red with black hairs, chocolate with tan, black with rust markings

Coat:
Short and smooth

Fun Fact!

Even though Miniature Pinschers resemble Doberman Pinschers, the breed actually comes from German Pinschers, Dachshunds, and Italian Greyhounds.

With ears that stand up high, pointed muzzles, and intense eyes, these alert, tough dogs are known for their unusually high walking style.

Mini Quiz

What is the Miniature Pinscher's country of origin?
A. England
B. Germany
C. Italy
(Answer on page 64)

Rottweiler

Height:
22–27 inches
Weight:
85–130 lbs

Group:
Working

Colors:
Black with reddish
to tan markings

Coat:
Medium-
length

Fun Fact!

The Rottweiler is considered a German breed, but it is most likely a descendant of the cattle dog brought by the Roman Empire in the 1st century AD.

Pup Personality

- obedient
- protective
- fearless

Sheepdog

Breed Details

Group: Herding
Height: 21 inches and up
Weight: 60 lbs and up
Coat: Long and coarse
Color: Light cream to white with gray, blue, or grizzle markings

Mini Quiz

True or false: Sheepdogs are shy and easy to train.
(Answer on page 64)

With a strong herding instinct, the shaggy Sheepdog is covered with long, wiry hair that often falls in front of its eyes.

Did You Know?

Sheepdogs have wiry coats that are prone to matting, so they need to be brushed at least once a week!

Weimaraner

Group:
Sporting

Height:
23-27 inches
Weight:
50-70 lbs

Coat:
Short and
smooth

Colors:
Gray, blue,
or silver

Fun Fact!

This dog's
nickname is
"The Gray
Ghost!"

The athletic weimaraner is graceful and friendly yet brave and alert, thanks to its roots as a hunting dog.

Based on its name, can you guess which European country this breed comes from? (Answer on page 64)

Mini Quiz

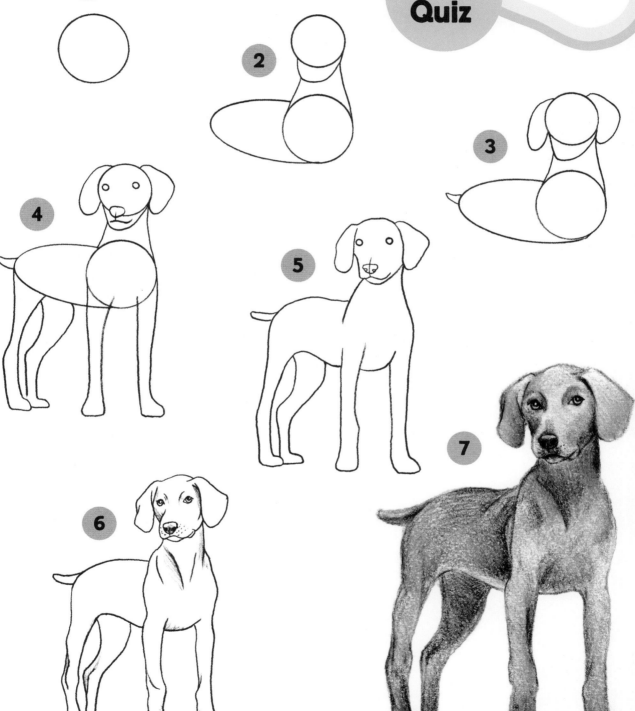

French Bulldog

Height:
12 inches
Weight:
28 lbs

Group:
Toy

Coat:
Short and
smooth

Colors:
Various combinations
of brindle, pied,
white, cream, fawn,
black, and gray

Fun Fact!

Frenchies were bred
down from the larger
English Bulldog in
the 1880s, first in
England and later
in France.

Sometimes called "Frenchies," French Bulldogs have compact bodies; wide faces; and rounded, bat-like ears.

Pup Personality

- energetic
- playful
- affectionate

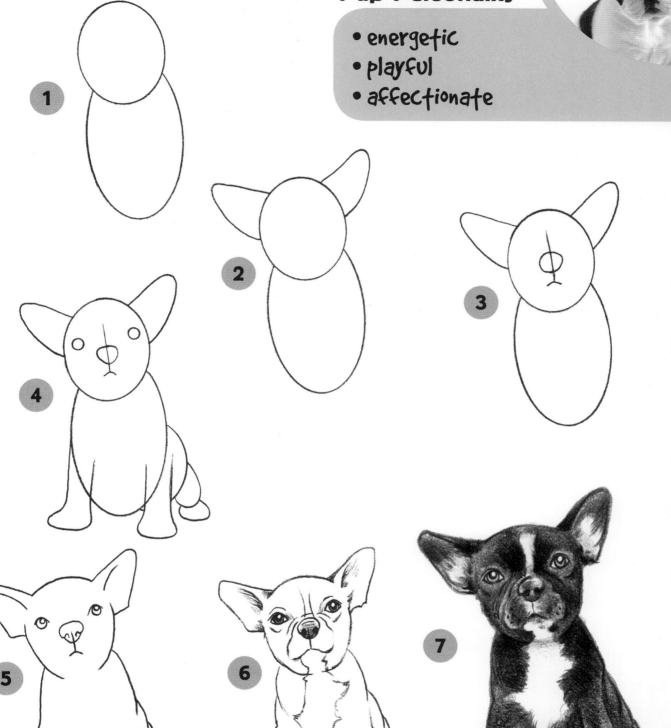

Collie

Breed Details

Group: Herding
Height: 22–26 inches
Weight: 50–70 lbs
Coat: Smooth (short and dense) or rough (long and fluffy)
Color: Combinations of white, tan, black, blue merle, and sable

Did You Know?

The Collie's long coat is fullest around the neck and chest, which is also called the "ruff." The long-haired breed is called "Rough," while the short-haired breed is called "Smooth."

These gentle, intelligent dogs are great with young children. They like being around people and other dogs.

True or false: Collies are often said to be "smiling." (Answer on page 64)

Mini Quiz

1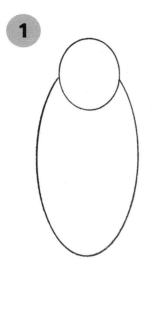

2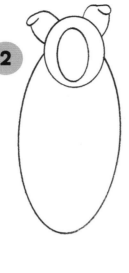

3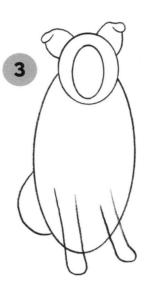

4

5

6

7

Great Dane

Breed Details

Group: Working
Height: 28–32 inches
Weight: 120–150 lbs
Coat: Short
Color: Black, fawn with a black mask, brindle with a black mask, blue-gray, harlequin, or mantle (dark areas over the back and sides)

Did You Know?

This breed is one of the tallest in the world. The tallest dog known to date was a Great Dane who stood 41 inches—just over 3 feet tall!

The Great Dane is the national dog of Germany. This massive, loyal companion is known for its size, but these dogs are also gentle and loving.

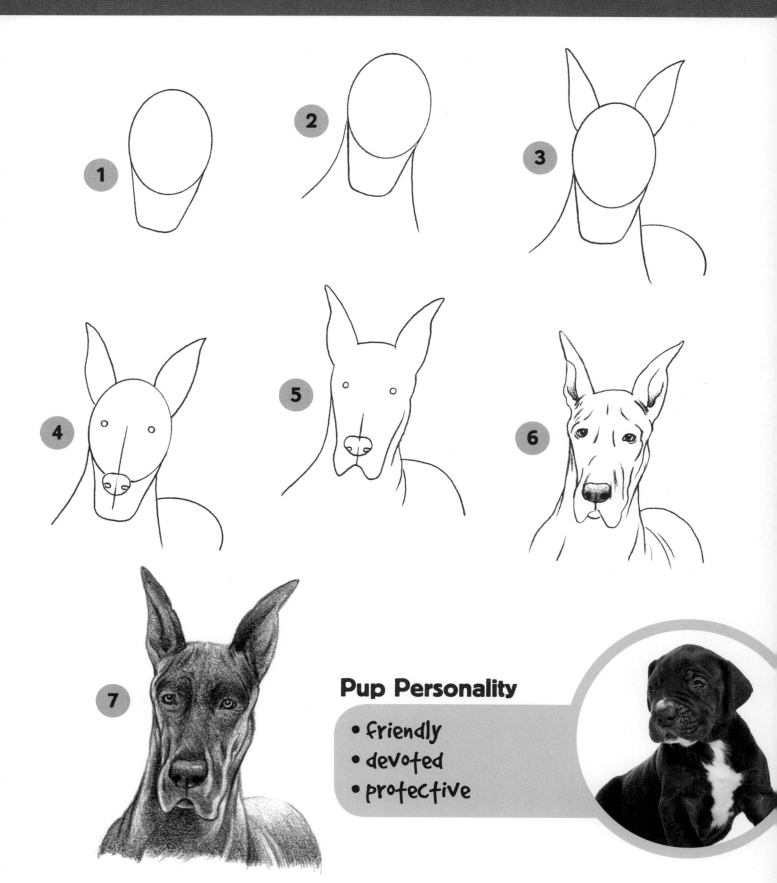

Pup Personality

- friendly
- devoted
- protective

Italian Greyhound

Height:
13–15 inches
Weight:
7–10 lbs

Group:
Toy

Coat:
Short and smooth

Colors:
Wide variety

Fun Fact!

Called the "IG" for short, Italian Greyhounds have a cat-like love of high places—they are often found perched on the backs of chairs, on windowsills, or any other high spot they can find!

This petite-boned breed may appear fragile, but these long-legged dogs are very athletic and limber.

Can you guess how old this breed is?
A. 400 years
B. 1,500 years
C. 2,000 years
(Answer on page 64)

Mini Quiz

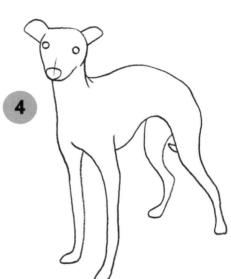

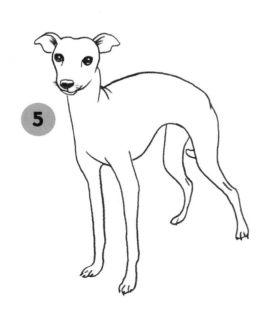

Mini Quiz Answers

Page 13: True. The spots on a Dalmatian don't grow in until a few weeks after birth. They continue to form until the dog is 6 months old.

Page 15: D. All of the above!

Page 17: Pomeranians are related to early sled dogs, the ancestors of the Husky.

Page 19: Snoopy, the mischievous dog belonging to Charlie Brown.

Page 29: True.

Page 39: True. Poodles are hypoallergenic dogs and have a non-shedding coat.

Page 43: C. Both. Huskies can have light blue eyes, brown eyes, one of each, or even parri-colored eyes: part blue and part brown.

Page 45: Red plaid—the same print that is found on many Scottish kilts!

Page 49: B. Miniature Pinschers were originally bred in Germany as rat hunters.

Page 52: False. These dogs love to be the center of attention. They are very stubborn and one of the most difficult breeds to train.

Page 55: Germany. Named after the German city of Weimar and one of its former dukes who enjoyed hunting.

Page 59: True. Part of its social nature, the Collie has a wide range of facial expressions.

Page 63: C. The Italian Greyhound has been around for 2,000 years.